POEMS
OF
THEMES AND UNITY

By
Anthony Panzardi

LEGAS

POEMS

OF

THEMES AND UNITY

Edited by J.A. Tully

Anthony Panzardi
Poems of Themes and Unity
ISBN 978-1881901-77-8

The author has also published two other books of poetry with Legas:

Auriga, Between Yellow Night and Refractive Sea, 1999;
Horologium, Beyond Tangible Dreams and Unconscious Walls, 2005.

For information and for orders, write to:

Legas

P.O. Box 149
Mineola, New York
11501, USA

3 Wood Aster Bay
Ottawa, Ontario
Canada K2R1D3

Legaspublishing.com

Contents

I

And then the seasonal green
Ascends in a simultaneous time.
Her eyes remain paused
Before the soft golden dawn.
An overwhelming light settles faintly
Upon her tender nape,
So still the roses break,
A matinal sound grows slowly
Over the midday fog,
And the recumbent petal
Compares quietly to her lips.
A sudden birth of mountain mist.

II

Warm day, dark and blue,
Nestles in the scent of deep tranquility.
Her arms extend graciously
Beneath the cerulean sky.
A rising heat forms wholeheartedly
Around silence and sounds.
Nature whispers below the passionate shade,
And she alludes voluptuously
To the tall meadow rue.
A whiteness, level with motion and wave.
A curling glow shy before the length of time.

III

The balance of woods and tone
Begins at the end of night.
The daffodils climb north
Around the stone-colored thaw.
Her tender thoughts mix among clusters of pine,
And the orb of day signals Earth
With patches of an albescent beam.
She privately returns to a height
Below the orange canopy.

IV

The circular pools, hazel in form,
Take heed to visions of cherry blossoms
And amorous scenes, as the snowy hills
Melt sensually below the peaks of white.
The summer sweetness bows toward
Her soft white skin.
Her hands, sheer as the rain,
Cup the ultimate breath,
Wet from the infinite drop, all unheard
Near curves in flocks and lakes.

V

And the meek horizon grows bold
Before the warm blue stream.
A sensual wind, barely felt
Above tint and ripple, excites the mind.
And the cherry tree displays an exquisite ripeness,
As she reclines in perfection
Atop the cool umber shade.
Her feminine composure delights my senses
Amidst the vast complexity of darkness and dawn.

VI

For the fair red petals
That fall beyond her reach,
I gladly collect the crimson flora,
As she smiles in the early morning warmth.
A tawny songbird chirps on the flowery bush,
And the dark green grass
Bends below the southern sky.
And with her fingers so fine,
She outlines my face,
While the sun casts a pale yellow glow.

VII

A white cloud skims the rim of the moon,
And the lake seems to move east
Like a silver liquid,
And I can sense her presence so near
At the end of the night.
Owls and crickets share the acoustic space,
And the dark fragrance of nature
Entices the newborn day.
She reminds me with a silent kiss.

VIII

Alas! The far end of the warm bright meadow,
Where I can see her soft image
Close to the large purple orchid,
Such a silence, as she moves forward
Like a vibrant ray of light.
The landscape bears resemblance to an ancient time.
The time combines both nature and reality.
And the natural pulchritude of life
Coincides with her unconditional beauty.

IX

Where have the peach trees grown?
It is now the warm season,
And she is delighted by the sweet midday nectar.
I travel quietly through the tall green grass,
A heavenly quest toward the visual feast.
She greets me with that succulent peach,
As her wet lips blossom
Against my unkempt cheek.
And moist pits blend below the massive bough.

X

Bright water, warm from the sun's orange rays.
The turquoise fish
Moves stealthily below the tiny swells
While she caresses the water
With the light on her dainty hands.
I follow her to the rosy liquid glare,
As the white-throated sparrow calls to its mate.
The simultaneous approach of ripples and song
Creates the ultimate ease
Among the bright beige sand.

XI

Nowhere does the hoary moonlight rest more beautifully
Than on her soft white breasts,
And the glistening mist rests upon the virgin's bower,
And the reason for a southern wind is unknown,
So she begins a timeless dance
That appears more like an aesthetic flow.
The dark silhouette of range and scope
Casts a background for her
In the pale blue darkness.

XII

Hungry bees settle upon the soft brown pollen.
A honey scent drifts from the inclined road.
And her laughter, like music,
Like nature, a symphony of solitude,
An avian choir, a solitary sound
Only for my ears,
And then the countless sounds of love
Beckoning the atmosphere,
Mixing the two among shades of green
And streams of white.

XIII

And the heavy bough, ripe with plums,
Rests in contrast against
The gray and white striated sky.
And I see her beautiful face
As if it were the unblemished portrait of nature.
At the slight curve and level plain,
She sits, with legs bare, reading old romantic verse
Under the sweet purple plums.
I know her well as she mouths the words
In perfect form of sound and tone.

XIV

We stretch near the tawny wall,
The brown ivy spreads like anatomical veins,
The wild strawberries pervade the atmosphere,
I kiss her shoulder,
I am warm from the eastern sun.
She holds her hand over the tiny white flowers
And says that the lightness is because
Of an immeasurable amount of hue.
We observe a melodious nest above the brown ivy.

XV

She appears as the sunrise,
And I walk toward the birth of day,
And the white oak shades the beautiful green path.
I listen to the silence form like a transparent mist,
The scent of bark overwhelms the cautious air,
The whole scene blooms from a golden bud,
And she quietly walks below
The remnants of a crimson sky,
Happy about the mixture of dusk with day.

XVI

What has the common redpoll left for our delight?
The twigs and vines from nature's seeds,
The hollow and leaves from vibrant trees,
And her only word is "yes"
As we pass the winding stream.
I witness her hand touch the purple-flowering raspberry
Then shyly stroke the moist purple lobes.
We count the five broad petals
And caress under nature's eye.

XVII

I cannot resist her, I must admit.
I tell it to the blackcap chickadee.
I tell it to the distant cloud.
She beckons me from the clear thin frost
As the smell of pine settles upon the amber soil.
I stop at an old gray log
Anticipating our intimate night,
And the palpable presence almost like a sheer season,
Far beyond the early hue.

XVIII

To me the moon is beautiful,
But it would be inferior to her gracious phase.
Ochre, off the still and colorless lake,
Reflects upon the great symmetrical stone.
And she begins to hum a lost sonata,
I recognize the mood,
The tempo coincides with rustic voices,
Choral wind, and the high pitch of flapping wings
Above the yellow grove.

XIX

She sits at the edge of the grassy earth,
Dangling her legs in the pond,
And the gleam declines from the turquoise dome,
Caressing the towering husk,
And the rain falls briefly and lightly
Over the leafy tops.
I kiss her warm wet thighs,
She smiles and reaches for the blackburnian warbler
As it disappears in the brush
Like a fine clear breeze.

XX

Countless times
The stars have decorated the infinite eve.
The white, silver, and pale blue dots
Remind her of our intimate bond and joyful thoughts
Of what shall come,
All in the heart.
She speaks to me from our long embrace,
"Oh, the sky has given us its white, silver,
And pale blue freckles of light."

XXI

A subtle bend of the fringed gentian in yellow shade,
And she, like a wallflower amidst the violet flame,
Bathes in the soft blue glare,
Inhaling the sweet scented air.
Behold her exquisite physique,
Nude behind that dark gray pine and scented shade.
I wait, since time becomes the essence of our love,
Of our being as one,
Like a trillion nocturnal suns.

XXII

Can we behave like the castaways of long ago?
Destined to relish the light green hills and dark blue lakes,
Recalling our primitive ways, sipping from winding
        streams,
Picking from the juicy growths,
Sleeping beneath the shaggy limbs,
All the day a tranquil show
From chipmunks, butterflies, and deer,
A progression of mute songs
Behind the elevated ground
As she appears like a summer morn.

XXIII

I see her gathering blueberries
Near the old stone schoolhouse.
I see her walking barefoot
Down the old dirt road.
With full basket and green bonnet,
She smiles at me and sits upon a shaded rock.
A young cardinal lands upon her tawny basket
And pecks at a large ripe blueberry.
I gaze again, as I have a thousand times before,
Enthralled by her angelic face.

XXIV

The month of autumn
Still brings in a dry comfortable warmth,
A slight sway of the willowy leaves,
And a long distant call from an avian roost,
And she knows that the yellow buds
Are behind the worn brown fence,
And I greet her passionately at the worn brown fence,
And we laugh and find many a rose,
Yellower than the eastern range of parallel light.

XXV

The morning overcast seems to twirl
Like a blue-gray galaxy,
And below in sight is the hill of grass and stone.
She meets me at the old wooden mill,
We begin our walk through the shades of fall,
Through the yellow and red spiral woods,
Through the brown and tan winding coves,
We embrace as the cool wind makes the autumn leaves
Dance around a dappled bark.

XXVI

The land, now, like a small sea of leaves,
And the rolling hills reflect a screened beauty
From the pale orange sun,
And she, engulfed in that serene setting,
Slowly becomes that screened beauty,
Changing the vast vision,
An unceasing part from sky to soil,
And behold the ruby-crowned kinglet,
Displaying a still-life pose and small red pate,
Anxious to partake in reflections of a serene setting.

XXVII

After our night, we stroll through the morning fog,
And I see her eyes so clear like a virgin lake,
So bright as the natural light
Peels the aerial cloak,
And she rests her head upon my shoulder
As we watch a viceroy flutter around a large brown stone
Damp with moss and dew.
She smiles ever so slightly
At that brief and simple movement,
And we observe with contentment.

XXVIII

We both see the pale blue star
Twinkling in the vast black sky.
We both huddle near the crackling flame.
The unknown star, so distant in the infinite night.
The fire growing, dancing in the air.
I touch the warm orange glow on her cheek,
She outlines my hand with her soft white fingers
As the mountain peaks appear to us
Like the beginning of the world,
And our only light enhanced by twigs and brush.

XXIX

She stops along the brook, admiring the marsh marigold
With its heart-shaped leaves and yellow flowers.
The wind is from the east,
And I can sense the spring
As it caresses the young green grass.
The purple finch lands between us,
And we both laugh with joy at its rosy head.
Even its breast has a tint of rose
As it moves almost undetectable
In the land of wood.

XXX

White-tailed deer are among the tawny reeds.
We are quiet and still.
She whispers into my ear
As dusk grows into a limpid gray.
Pine needles blanket the soft ground.
A seasonal odor emitting from beneath our feet.
It is a faint fragrance
Like fruit from distant fields.
A white grove bending to the habitat
Or quiet and still like the tawny reeds
And white-tailed deer.

XXXI

Behold her most fair above all exquisite things,
As with the ripe yellow sun or thick red petals,
While the hills naturally form a rare observation
Of swells and indentations,
And sight abounds across the circular setting,
Even the red-tailed hawk
Glides as if in an infinite vision,
Making an aerial path high above our heads,
And we sit on the patch of earth
Communicating our thoughts.

XXXII

The pleasant scent of cedar in the cold afternoon
Drifts subtly between town and thickets.
The fox sparrow busy, away from its dwelling.
A rusty brown color
Against the dark gray barn.
And I walk from the light brown fence
To the sky-blue lake,
And I can still smell the cold cedar,
And I can still see the rusty brown bird,
And she walks with me throughout.

XXXIII

The sun today is magnificent,
It is an orb of red,
It bathes the ivory clouds and fertile earth.
And the water, some still, some moving,
At times like rock, at times like smoke,
A symbol of life, a drop upon the meadowsweet,
A great silvery-blue,
Level with the mountain base,
Level below the golden-crowned kinglet,
And the breeze stirs a paper birch leaf,
And I find her on the wooden porch and crimson heat.

XXXIV

What do the woodland beasts reveal in the darkest nights?
The shadowy forms move, then rest
Under the full-white moon.
The temperature is dropping from the northeast air.
We see naked eyes reflecting like silver stones
Or like tiny stars among the timbered gardens.
And she asks me to look deeper into the optic black
As we pause, joyfully, in the pool of light,
Grateful for the darkest night.

XXXV

My heart feels as nature feels,
The pressure of life, the beauty of life,
The formation of the towering peaks,
The formation of the glacier lakes,
Our hearts can perceive residue of distant years,
And we feel the formation of life,
And she rubs the moisture and sand into my palm,
And I feel the pressure as glorious as nature,
As human as the heart,
As a boundless past for two.

XXXVI

The pond on the southern end
Has a dark yellow tint from the newly born pollen,
A mild wind carries the golden dust from flowering
                    plants,
And a praying mantis clings motionless to an emerald
                    reed,
And we walk up the inclined path,
Seeing the great brownish-gray barks,
Feeling the dry comfortable heat,
And she points down to the American redstart,
As the mild wind shifts up the inclined path.

XXXVII

She walks over the twigs and leaves
In another October day,
Soft, cool, and gray.
I hear footsteps, and I see many small spaces of sky
Between thin dappled branches,
The sound much nearer now,
And she has the red maple leaves cupped in her delicate
                    hands,
One by one we observe the colors, the patterns, the shapes,
Each one unique
Like snowflakes or human thoughts.

XXXVIII

The moon is out,
But the sky is still a pale blue
And the hills are still a pale red,
And the night patiently waits to descend,
A gradual process as fish settle and mammals scurry,
And her voice is distinct
As the transition is finally made,
Her clear shadow, shapely in the last moments of light,
No blackness in comparison,
No particle of day to compare,
Only a vision of shadow so fair.

XXXIX

Near the farm, over a small wooden bridge,
We see an ermine, brown, with a black-tipped tail,
It moves quickly behind the yellow birch.
I tell her to watch near the claw-like roots,
As it walks with a quick pace
Over the small red bridge.
And the farmer takes off his hat and waves
With brown hat still in hand,
And we wave back from the red wooden bridge.

XL

It is close to the end of another daylight,
And the snow falls in a pure restless flurry.
The snow seems more like rain,
But it is white, not clear,
And she says to me,
"Only the brightest stars can be seen tonight."
I realize this because of all the white anxious specks
Decorating the blue-black sky,
Until that orange star ascends
For another birth of day.

XLI

The cherry trees grow between the dense brown field
And green oval marsh.
The deep red fruit
Gives the land a productive spread,
And the whole hue of green, red, and brown
Embraces the morning chill
As four crows fly in the western view.
And we wander among the trees like children in a maze
Picking up the fallen fruit
And admiring the beauty of the ripe red limbs.

XLII

How many times does that southern star flicker
In its chronological life?
Its name is still unknown,
But its presence is known to us
And to all who observe it,
Like a tiny pearl dancing in that infinite space,
Giving us thought and amazement.
"Look at it flicker once more," she said,
Knowing the great vitality it takes
To dance on uncharted time,
And this southern star has a history of curious observers.

XLIII

We see a dense green islet
On this vast blue lake,
And we see a tiny red house
On the shore of this dense green islet,
But nothing stirs there,
The water is calm,
And the tranquility is as natural as the air we breathe,
And we turn for a moment
To see a spotted salamander,
Only to disappear under the wet brush.
A green bird stirs the tiny islet.

XLIV

Was it a dream that the soft orange sky
Beheld my thoughts
Until the silent rain performed its spontaneous ode?
I sleep as a living thing,
Naked and human,
Eyes moving and observing,
Sensing the clean high peak air,
Waiting for the dream to signal a palpable touch,
And I can feel her warm skin against mine,
Two humans blending as mind and body,
Waiting for the return of the silent rain.

XLV

A beige wooden sailboat
Adrift on the western side of the lake.
The wind is mild,
And a few high clouds move west to east.
A man and a woman relax on deck,
Looking east at the puffy white clouds.
We stand at the far side of the path that ends,
Pebbles and dirt make a new path,
And we continue our journey,
Still looking at the western side of the lake.

XLVI

At the time,
When there is a slight tint of white to be seen,
I hear the whistle from a bird of prey,
And then I see it glide above the bare treetops,
Floating in a small hemisphere,
Slowly disappearing over the brown jagged hills.
The sounds of the east are different today
Than the silence of the west
As the day slowly begins
Then ends over the brown jagged hills.

XLVII

The April thaw transforms the landscape from white
                    to brown,
And the melting becomes clear thin streams,
And the thick roots of great trees
Inhale the cool moist soil.
The horned lark checks the ground for insects and grass,
But near the rustic barn,
There are still a few patches of that wintry white,
As a wary chipmunk peaks its tiny head
Through a hole from an old gray stump.

XLVIII

She reclines in the east
Near the eastern bluets
Reading her favorite book of poems,
Repeating the verse in a low musical tone,
Repeating the sound in a voice for early day,
And she is the morning,
And she is the peak of the sun,
And the day moves into a great sphere,
Balancing the reflections of the turquoise air,
Balancing the east and the west,
And her reflection is morning.

XLIX

It has always been an ancient melody,
The day as a whole,
The green buds open wide,
Strange and familiar songs emit from quiet trees,
The northern flora, a light-green from an avian view,
And the land's soft vibrations
Penetrate the fallen seeds,
And the flower has a purpose,
And the redbird has its northern view,
And the mammals tread softly
Permeating the fallen seed.

L

She is more beautiful today than yesterday's dawn,
And tomorrow will bring that golden glare,
And she will follow along the path
Of the fragrant water lily,
And tomorrow will bring that sweet smell
Of the warm August lake
As it leaks through the massive gray rocks
Trickling into her hand,
Her palm wet, glistening in the golden glare,
And I pass that sweet smell,
Touching the palm of her hand
As if it is tomorrow's dawn.

LI

We are most humble
Toward the mountains and the night.
We grow dark
Into that palpable night.
She feels my heart beating against her heart.
She feels the pulsing heat against her breasts.
We are humble under the invisible moon,
A midnight moon, round, black, mysterious,
Like the black mountains, elusive to the human heart,
And the humble heart beats quietly
Under the dominant night and gentle embrace.

LII

Where the gray fox hunts
The twilight opens its eyes,
And the stars are like white pupils
Observing the smallest of life,
Observing the blue peak hills and black hollow tree,
And the gloam observes all of nature's needs,
And the small cedar house settles in the highest woods
Emitting a scent of birch
In the form of a birdlike smoke,
Unheard, unseen,
Overlapping the time of one day to the next.

LIII

The snow fell heaviest on the western hills,
And the great mounds are like ivory billows
Inflating with whiteness
As the sky drops its feathery frost,
And on the northern rocks
The rough hills become smooth from the silvery ice,
A smooth frost bending over the ridged landscape,
And the snowshoe hare
Becomes part of the white-ridged landscape,
Except for its black-rimmed ears
Which can be seen from the southern hills.

LIV

A few days before spring,
The wind blew with an ancient reminder,
But the day that follows
Is destined to repeat its extraordinary tranquility,
And the spring days are the aboriginal buds
Of the red and yellow fields,
And the green land, saturated with season,
Becomes life of the interval,
And incessant interlude,
Bringing forth a vision of color,
And the last fir needle
Before the countless intervals of summer.

LV

The rain smells sweet,
And we can see from an inclined spot
That the rain has stopped,
But the wetness makes for memorable thoughts.
The leafless trees produce a lovely sight on a secluded
                 spot,
The low bark appears to be a dark gray,
And the high bark appears to be a deep blue,
The changing sky makes for that lovely sight,
And we move inward for a closer look.

LVI

How was this reddish rock created?
How did it part from the rose-covered cliffs?
How did it part from the earth's auburn crust?
When did the water meet the earth
At the base of the lake?
And could these clouds have been present
At the time of the last formation?
The clouds melt in the distance,
And a new shape designs the light-blue sky,
The seasonal part of a new formation.

LVII

The lake trout are active,
Swimming below the quivering glare,
And the bent shadow
Keeps the fish in a strong purple glare,
The ripples break,
Then lap the pointed stones,
The wood thrush, unseen,
Only a far flute sound over the pastured ground,
And in many a day,
The shadowy stones reflect the last slice of glare,
Keeping the warmth active,
Until the many become the beauty of the few.

LVIII

Red meadow, red morning bird, her lips red,
Her white breasts bare before the yellow sun,
A scattering of yellow on white wings,
And we wander peacefully
On the yellow hills and on the green earth,
And when she is here,
All things to me are serene,
And the calmest things of all are at her fingertips,
Touching my vastness,
Her entire beauty in the meadow,
Touching the immaculate red.

LIX

A horizontal scent follows the black night,
And the night sky watches over life's slumber,
And nature has its way,
Creating a constant image,
Creating a prehistoric breeze,
The new wilderness, the splintered light
Filtering through long, long ago,
A prehistoric light permeating through eyes, moon, and
        sky,
Reaching to the unseen beauty,
Creating the heart for a tree, veins for the sun,
And the image of beauty over the prehistoric slumber.

LX

Pine siskin,
And a subtle flight into a coniferous phase,
Like the phases of Venus,
Like the phases of the moon,
Like the hue-changing rind,
The climate pattern unpredictable from the beginning,
From the first phases of life,
From the origin of summer fronds or winter flakes,
And much of time still in its original phases,
As the caterpillar transforms, or the orange and black
        butterfly
Lands on the crescent-shaped light.

LXI

I feel her warm mouth
On my shaded eye,
And I feel the warm light
Engulfing the shaded earth,
And the blue-green life,
Extolling the atmosphere in a timeless setting,
Breathing in the realm of a boundless season.
And one day the shade will become white,
And the white will become yellow,
And the yellow will become a shade of brown, orange,
               and red,
And the seasons, four and many,
Will become life's breath.

LXII

Today the lake looks like an ocean,
And the mountains look like an oil painting,
And we walk through the interior,
And she said in her sweet voice,
"This tree has the most beautiful pears,
And the amber boughs bear the succulent fruit."
We partake in its juicy flesh,
Sitting with our backs
Against the dun-colored bark,
Watching the blue harebells
Nodding in the western field.

LXIII

Up above the small green hill,
A coyote scavenges in the cool moist thicket,
And the temperature, now at dusk,
Drops below the morning low,
And this dog-like beast,
Subtle as the transition of twilight,
Wails at the pale yellow moon,
As it did since the last sunless time,
And no one can hear the primitive speech,
Only the full moon can be heard
With all its sublimity behind the crimson clouds.

LXIV

The stone cottage is nestled deep
In the February woods,
A white dust covers the roof,
Birch burning in the hearth,
The white smoke is visible in the dark blue night,
And Sirius, so far from our sun,
Twinkles bright,
Like a pale blue sun-dot,
So far from our moon, so far from our thoughts.
Yet, one can imagine its closeness,
Its hot dim light,
Bluer than the bluest night.

LXV

The August sundrops
Bloom on the day's peak,
And the ground beetle moves back and forth
On the heated soil,
And the sailboats float east,
No great wind,
A light breeze over the glistening green surface,
And the children play on the southern end of the sand,
Running to the northern rocks,
Watching the August lake,
A great breeze over stagnant ponds and thread-like
                     branches,
A slight cooling over the northern sand.

LXVI

The brown ivy climbs the old gray fence,
And the old farmer is content with his fence,
And he is proud of the growth of his farm,
And the spring beauty,
With its pink petals,
Attracts the young brown deer
Walking cautiously near the old gray fence.
And from east to west the warm rain falls,
Soaking the four young deer,
But they are content with the rain
And the old gray fence.

LXVII

Nature beckons the life of the sun
And all its splendor,
And I hear a soft voice amid the sugar maple,
As a wind of light
Hurls against the gray bark,
And we lie in the light's splendor
Watching the tree's crest brush the infinite sky,
And we beckon the moonlight,
I can see her, and I can touch her,
And a soft pale heat melts between our bodies,
And the night's light answers our call.

LXVIII

Night,
Like celestial lamps,
Fen and pebbles,
Two lights, from the moon, from Venus,
Pale orange, milk-white,
The night beaming with a beautiful pale light,
A soft grayness reflecting from the sky lamps,
Reflecting the eyes of a great horned owl,
And the night eyes blinking and twinkling,
Continuously, not knowing the seconds, the centuries,
Knowing the inevitable beauty,
For the absence of time.

LXIX

Dark gray branches
Over the freshwater stream.
Light gray conifers
Embraced by a seasonal burst.
Rows and rows of trees
Letting in the variegated gleam,
A rebirth into the halls of light,
Fairer than branches in the southern wood.
And behold! A pileated woodpecker
With its jungle call and carmine crest,
Pecking and tapping like an avian drum,
Echoing against the rows of variegated trees,
Bringing the early morning, its musical life.

LXX

Wildlife,
Earth's menagerie.
Black star covered with light.
Mammals and reptiles move on the pliable earth.
And at dusk,
The water level is as high as the reptile's tongue.
And at dawn,
The water level is as low as the mammal's tracks.
And the box turtle moves east toward dawn,
And the porcupine moves west toward dusk,
But birds and insects fly, north and south,
Above the water.

LXXI

Time,
If the voice of a light-year could speak,
Spreading a great light, a great distance,
Sending an articulate light to our small blue world,
Reaching the depths of nature
With the precise shades of hue,
With the precise shade of frost and dew,
With the same light
As trillions of miles or a solitary star,
And the land and sky
Uttering the sound of presence,
Shedding the perpetual light of time.

LXXII

And the old couple sit on their sunlit porch,
Thinking of yesterday,
Thinking of tomorrow.
It is, now, late spring,
And they think of summer, autumn, and winter,
And they think of their seasonal guests,
And the old couple greet the outdoor guests,
They welcome the tall yellow blooms,
The brown and orange leaves,
The soft white hills,
And the young couple walk through the sunlit fields,
Thinking of tomorrow.

LXXIII

The sun's beauty rests upon my eyes,
And I feel its yellow strength
Deep within my face,
And I see her in a coral dress, sheer,
Against the yellow leaves,
And her body, beautiful, white,
Against the orange light,
Her voice sounds like summer,
Our love sounds like poetry,
And she appears to me like the sky and the earthly hue,
A vision of that beauty among the summer verse.

LXXIV

Land,
And vegetal peaks of the mountain,
Grand green flowers
Dropping wetness on Earth's pores,
And the clouds, amid peak and sky,
With dark gray bottom,
Pass quietly through the midday dimness,
As the heavy flowers nod with the midday rain,
And a thin shimmering flow meets the shaded ravine,
Carrying the twigs, leaves, and bark,
Carrying the dark gray bottom of saturated clouds.

LXXV

Anytime, any season,
I love to hear the beautiful sound
Of an unknown bird.
I think it is orange or scarlet.
I think it sounds like the day being born.
I think the tree has a scarlet season.
I think the mountain has an orange tone.
And two leaves touch,
Tree to tree,
And one bird flies between the unknown season,
And the beautiful sound echoes from the two trees.

LXXVI

Tall crystal trees,
Amber below the shooting star.
The cold white night,
White hills against black night,
And the cold black sky
Shows its incandescent tail to the sleepy winter town.
The glowing white streak heats the frozen sky,
And people observe with wonder from their wooded
                abodes,
Fixing their eyes to the heavens through frosted panes,
Pondering with the indoor warmth
Under heavy white roofs,
But time has dissolved the glowing heat
And pictorial whiteness.

LXXVII

She embraces me with naked arms
Below the olive-green moon.
What sweet beauty she sets upon my heart,
What sweet words she feeds my mind,
What sweetness the surrounding flora makes
As we unfold the virgin night,
Exploring our flesh, our shades,
Layer by layer, the many shades of night,
The shades of stars and planets alike.
And now the moon rises above us
Into a grayish-white.

LXXVIII

Vision of water, clear,
The beautiful horizon, hazy,
And boat, raising its white sail,
Sailing on the sea-green lake
As if it is on an ocean or a sea,
Heading west into the setting sun,
And the pale red sun, half visible, half fading,
Fading into a watery mirror,
Where all reflections wiggle black and gold,
And the tiny boat, like a sea-green shark,
White fin, slowly sailing in hazy visions of west.

LXXIX

Trout lily, bronze and yellow.
Garter snake slides along the moist undergrowth.
The black swallowtail investigates
The warmth of the bronze and yellow light.
The warmth spreads like roots and veins
Among the lower valley,
And the thunder echoes the upper valley,
And the sound spreads like color over the foggy range.
A weak storm, brief, passes through
The thick of trees like a clear color.
A vague moisture lingers through the warm light.

LXXX

The grayish-brown day
Blends into the old windmill.
The morning dove,
With its cooing call and whistling wings,
Follows an inclined path, turns east,
And lands upon the old windmill.
The climate, motionless,
The grayish-brown dove, still,
But the weather vane moves west, slightly.
Time makes the day almost unnoticeable
Like the motion of whiskers on the sly nocturnal beast,
But the motionless eyes blend conspicuously into the
                    wind.

LXXXI

Life and heart,
Nature's heart is its flora and fauna,
And my heart is a piece of life,
The clouds, the soil, the water,
And our hearts throb among the mist,
Like fire, like melody, like the first world reflection,
And we make love among the golden reeds,
And her heart and life are the naked mist,
And the reflections cast the beautiful beginnings
Of tranquil lakes, rain clouds, and abundant earth.

LXXXII

Can it be Uranus,
A pale greenish dot in that black distance,
Barely visible to the naked eye?
Can it be that tiny pale disk?
Can it be Neptune or the formation of a mortal star?
And can the black distance
Show its trillion white lights?
The world has its own light.
The world has its own blackness.
And life exists among the two,
They evolve beautifully into a mortal gray.

LXXXIII

The tree swallow looks from tree to sun
And from sun to tree.
The barn owl looks from barn to moon
And from moon to barn.
Birds in flight look toward the heavens.
Early plants grow beneath the empty perch,
And the deep winding stream, flowing west,
Breaking against the smooth brown rocks,
And the river otter, wingless,
Looks toward the heavens,
But the landscape, today,
Has a lovely blue tint from any observation.

LXXXIV

After the heavy rains,
The saturated earth becomes heavy with mud,
And once again, the rains come,
Then the dry days turn the mountainous land
Into a pyramid-like crust,
With pools of beige water forming on low-level paths,
Then drying in the April sun.
And the bullfrog, with its low mournful croak,
Hops through the evening crust
And seeks the eastern pond.
Now mud and crust bear an arboreal life.

LXXXV

She asks for the blue light
Upon the naked Earth,
I give her my reflection
From the clear morning sky,
And I love the soft eastern hue,
And I can see the sky's light in her beautiful eyes,
And the depth of blue
Pervades all the interior hills,
And she becomes the soft eastern hue.
I look for the early morning planet,
I know it has returned among the soft blue glare.

LXXXVI

And suddenly she appears
Among the sparkling light of the green pasture.
I walk a great distance between the sycamore trees.
Her small figure becomes clearer and brighter.
I pass a northern oriole
Perching on a large flaking branch.
She is, now, close enough
That I can see her radiant smile.
I pass a red squirrel
As it looks for seeds and buds.
She is here, and we meet
In the sparkling light of the green pasture.

LXXXVII

Pioneers once walked Earth and woods.
The circle of trees makes a natural orbit
For early morning birds.
And the pioneers saw the woods,
Yellow with day,
Black with night.
Now we see the woods, winter white,
A cold white blanket in mid-December,
Where the pioneers would leave tracks on virgin snow,
And the late autumn ice
Would coat the long slender branches,
And now we see the winter tracks.

LXXXVIII

Light! The bright beauty!
Why do you cast a golden complexion
On the face of Earth?
Why do you bathe us with moonlight?
Even in rain you send us a luminous bolt.
And we thank you with green leaves and orange petals,
And we thank you with the yellowness
Reflected on the great stones,
And you display the ultimate blue light,
Disguised at times in seasons,
But as a vast, unconditional gift.

LXXXIX

Silver dew speckles the bunchberry.
A grasshopper slowly eats a brown stalk.
But above the cloud cover,
The heavens grow inward and outward.
The energy throbs with color, sound, and endlessness.
The ageless black bursts silently,
Creating its own finitude,
Creating its own beauty,
Creating its own colorless light,
And the young Earth compares to the ageless beauty,
And compares to the silver dew and brown stalk.
The old Earth sheds its age.

XC

The mist looks like white smoke,
Thick white mist
Ascending from the bark-like mountains,
Straight, slow, upward,
Like a snow geyser in an early spring morning.
The air is uncertain,
Rising in an early April day.
And now, the water vapor has a light brown tint,
Mirrored from the mountain's face.
The day is still early,
And four gray birds appear then disappear
Between the smoke and the mist.

XCI

Her mouth is like a rose,
And on the soft petals by the lake
Is where we love,
And the crimson sun is like a rose,
And the moon is very low, almost indiscernible,
And there are other suns in other galaxies,
Extremely faint and very high,
Stars, almost detectable on this warm summer day,
They are the suns of their galaxies
And the stars to us,
And we compare petals and suns.

XCII

In a region where the summer held brown and green,
The children now play in the snowy drifts,
And they pretend, in the white of day,
To be the settlers from time long ago,
When the northern drifts mounted high,
And wildlife was more than plenty,
And nature's white rind, so soft and cold,
Yields the beautiful brown and green flesh,
And the children, at the far end of the playful region,
Become tomorrow's settlers.

XCIII

How do the creatures of day
Compare to the voices of night?
How does the lost breeze sound to the missing leaves?
When does the last bluebird exit its boundless light?
The vague dense light mimics an avian voice,
And the hot black night harbors the folded wings,
And the creatures of night
Leave their breath as prints
Against the pure black sky,
And the day sounds like the present breeze in solitude.

XCIV

The sun and the rain
Lure me into the vast composure.
The pebbles and the wind remain invisible.
A sudden movement from the elliptical leaves.
She wears the sunshine, beautifully,
Like soft yellow skin.
She wears her nakedness
Like the rain and the sun.
She wears the flower in her hair.
I see the rain glistening on her legs.
I see the fragmental light in the sun-soaked rain,
Shapely and neat.

XCV

Tonight we love,
And tomorrow a blue bouquet will scent the sky,
And the green water fish
Will swim under the rising scent,
A flute-like voice will pass through the leafy limbs,
The day's end will begin
With the last moments of a warm wind.
The time pattern breaks into a fragrant color,
A lovely distinction between two resonant days,
And tomorrow night,
We will feel the invisible scent.

XCVI

Flowers face the scattered rocks,
The flowery rocks cover the brown light,
And the strangers walk among the shaded roses.
They stop at the meadow's edge.
They observe a brown thrasher
Rustling through the brittle leaves.
They continue toward the quiet town
Looking for other strangers to meet,
Looking for the few, the palpable light,
The interior beauty, a particle of the natural creation.
The strangers realize and coincide with Earth.

XCVII

The mountain appears as a hill.
The giant bird appears as a speck.
I see the speck move across the hill.
Could it be the golden eagle?
Could it be an unknown species?
The height is level with wing and hue,
The brown earth is elevated with shrubs and rock,
The great distance narrows with a leafy bronze
And widens in the bluish-white,
But the early scope agrees with the legendary appearance.

XCVIII

The earthworms,
The solar eclipse,
The children's laughter,
All present together in time,
And all the familiar eyes watch
The ancient drones and phonetic chirps,
And the sunlit moon
Keeps its face to our world,
And the voice of a howl speaks to the human
Just before the rise of day,
Or the moon's side of the cloud moves east
Toward a brighter sound or a brighter diversity.

XCIX

She meets me here
At the autumn stone.
She wears her cloak and bonnet.
I kiss her cheek and take her hand.
The wind blows through our fingers and eyes.
We hear a distant veery
Among the orange and brown patches of wind.
We taste the October wind
As it ends abruptly in the November sun.
With a sun such as this,
We can feel the brown and orange face of this stone.

C

The dirt road was once a botanical path,
And the treetop was once a towering shade,
And the old farmer tends to the earth,
He feeds the earth with seed,
His tan hands turn the brown soil,
And the morning sky is calm
With white, yellow, and blue,
And the midday sky is thick and heavy
With gray, purple, and blue.
The rain falls lightly onto the earth.
The farmer knows this was once
A botanical shade.

CI

Is it Mars,
High in the western sky,
Or a cool star,
That appears somewhat reddish
With the black and twinkling night?
And the perception is quite clear,
With a few low clouds moving east to west.
And the west,
Still vaguely red and beautiful,
Displays this planet or this reddish sun.
And the wooded night
Is so distant in sight, but not in time,
And the earthly space divides its dark and light.

CII

Nature of the world
Or the nature here.
The stone of the world
Or the stone here.
Anterior fog around the pre-dawn beast.
Peripheral vision of the world
Or peripheral vision here, in the mind.
And we think our pre-dawn thoughts,
And we settle here, among nature,
Among the post-dawn world,
Among the red pine.
And the pre-world senses will last
Until the beasts fade among the peripheral world.

CIII

Her fingers,
Wet from the stream,
Palm dripping, eyes dreaming.
She holds her hair bunched above her shoulders.
The silvery water flows gently
Over the grayish-blue rocks.
I join her at the water's edge,
The sun joins her at the stream.
The rocks begin to twinkle white,
And I cup the stream and the sun in my palms,
And I give her all their reflections,
And I give her all their mirrored beauty.

CIV

Could it be the elusive lynx
Or the tawny ghost in the wooded mist?
White tracks, white undergrowth,
The wintry phase has a light gray tint
Against the ulterior hills.
The shadowy white trees, still, like marble statues.
Crystal gray wings flapping in the stillness.
Pale yellow sun shining at its farthest point.
The forest frost absorbs the faint yellow heat,
And the January light, like a pallid lamp,
Struggles through the stony limbs.

CV

The old woman attracts the hummingbirds
With her cardinal flowers,
And the old man gazes into the lovely blue
As he pulls water from the well.
The morning hour has given a chill
To this August day.
And the afternoon brings a warmth
From beyond the southern elms.
The old couple relax in the early twilight heat.
There is still enough day to clearly see
The tall gray elms.
They can hear the soft swaying of the highest leaves.

CVI

The moon is waning tonight,
But yesterday it was ripe and full
Like a coral fruit,
And tomorrow it will be like dark wings to the mind.
The beauty of flight,
Thoughts of an eclipse, reddish and black,
Visions from Earth,
White clouds over shadowy prey.
The soft black moon, full and ripe,
Sets in the west.
The beauty of dark mornings,
Thoughts of a rising day, yellow and blue.

CVII

Pollen falling from the sky
Looks like snow falling from the trees.
Small yellow flakes whirl around
Like a golden squall,
Covering the warm sunny roofs,
And the homes, deep among the listless leaves,
Of wood or stone,
Share the same snowy grain,
And the meadowlark sings into the powder-blue sky,
And all the people call themselves settlers of Earth,
They observe the brown active soil, the cloudless rain,
And the pure pollination.

CVIII

The lake is blue,
But the sun makes it appear yellowish-green,
And the rocks below the tenuous waves are greenish-blue.
The rowboat leaves a dark rippling tail.
Two butterflies, small and white,
Graze the north and the heavens.
Two birds, small and black,
Graze the south and Earth.
And all the birds and all the butterflies soaked in light
Beat their wings over the shaded lake.
The blue water speaks to the hoary wings.

CIX

Melting light on frozen lake,
Nighttime over the frost-covered town,
White woods near the white town,
Town and woods under solid white rain,
The heavy snow, wet, dense, on trees and homes,
Gray deer wander from woods to town,
Children dream of themselves in a distant land,
Playing under the warm white sun,
Acting like the golden eagle
Over the cold green trees,
And the last sound of the day
Imitates the melting night.

CX

And she comes to me lighthearted.
And she comes to me with laughter.
We take heed to the sound of a bird call,
So exact to its last treetop song,
So precise is the mountain sound,
Settling, again, after thousands of years,
And I listen to the silence of the sun
Rotating on its axis,
And I listen to the silence of the soil
Growing under the rainstorm,
And she is everything I hear.

CXI

Look at Venus over the twilight lake
As its clouds reflect the light of the sun,
But it is third, in brightness,
Only to the sun and the moon.
It is beauty,
But to me she is the beauty on Earth,
Naked among clouds and light,
Her eyes wet, bright, tears of happiness.
I touch her tears with my lips,
And she lays her breasts upon my beating heart.

CXII

The strangers wave
On top of the sun-covered hill.
They wave at us in the partial light.
They smile at the sun.
We see them picking flowers,
White ones, pink ones, orange ones,
On the bottom of the hill.
They walk from the green land to the naked trees.
We see them plant the natural hues,
While the beautiful browns and grays constantly drip
And become a permanent shape.

CXIII

Why does the forest in the north
Look different from the flowers in the east?
Why does the sky in the east
Look different from the clouds in the north?
And why is this earthy aroma
Level with the empyreal scent?
A distance from sight,
The fish swim, partly in water, partly in air,
The vast little waves are like tiny crystal peaks,
And the whole southern sight
Reaches into a meadowland,
Penetrating the north and the east.

CXIV

Horse and carriage on this pavement.
The scene becomes the nineteenth century.
The sound is from the edge of town.
Light and breeze drift across the beautiful white horse.
The pale gray overcast makes this splendent lake
Look like a chestnut sea,
A soft reddish-brown, shimmering silver and white.
The scene becomes oil on canvas.
The sound echoes from the town of stone and wood
To the land of rocks and trees.

CXV

See the few marking their scent,
And see the red fox as plain as the surroundings,
As obscure as the bear, black against the white pine,
And hear the woodchuck, close but out of sight,
And hear the simple sound of water
Falling from above or the complexity of a red stone,
Or the days after each day,
A rose will look as beautiful as a stone,
And the days of tomorrow
Will gather each piece of light.

CXVI

Clouds and leaves
Are the pieces of the trees and the sky.
And the hills behind us are green and orange
Like the day.
The summer day, with its morning heat,
Reclines our hearts and our bodies
Between those clusters of time.
And her arms hang white over my naked shoulders.
Her legs, beautiful, shapely,
Shaded by the untouched light,
And I rest my cheek upon her thigh.

CXVII

The wind calls down the nocturnal beast,
It circles the gray mountain
Disguised as an avian ghost.
The season shakes the sky into a cylindrical storm,
And the thunder beats the light
Like a celestial drum,
And the gray mountain sheds its wind,
Its growth is in disarray,
But tranquility circles in green,
A year or hours before the season returns,
With wind as calm as exhaling
Through the southern peaks.

CXVIII

They say it is Saturn in the southern horizon,
But it looks like a tiny yellow star.
Where are its beautiful rings?
Where will it be tomorrow
When the moon is in its crescent phase?
Where will it be
When the brightness intensifies
On the deep black hills?
And many ravens fly among the oak,
Spreading out like black haze,
Weaving into the wooded fabric.
They say the oak is black,
But it looks like the shadow of Saturn's rings.

CXIX

The grains of sand are pale compared to the white rocks,
And today,
The pioneers remember the scent of
Stars, fire, and water,
They feel the slightest change in color,
No timepiece, no compass,
No change in the voiceless air,
But the bending rocks change under the granular scent,
A lost trail,
As vast as the four-footed tracks,
Appears at the edge of the night,
And the pioneers plan, from memory,
To survive the slightest change.

CXX

She had fallen asleep under the bright open leaves,
And I wake her
Before the blackbirds circle the murmuring trees.
She had been dreaming
On the day of the dark yellow light.
She said her dreams are the landscapes of life,
The piecemeal of beauty,
And our love as one
Among the clear and infinite few,
And we know the few as
Sparkling drops from star-like clouds,
Sun-colored wind,
And the day after the dream.

CXXI

This unmeasured land
Of gold grass and stony curves
Separates at the north end.
The stone-shaped pond stretches white
Below the nine loons,
And wave-like curves bounce their cries
Into a shallow cloud.
A slight orange protrusion from the east
Inspires the quiet surface life
And signals the active depth.
The flat glaze rises like vertical spots,
A beginning for the rest to dominate or neglect
The indication and the hidden marks.

CXXII

Children frolic
And unmask the sky and the bark.
They dance in the corner of an autumn rainbow.
The playground is the imaginary Earth,
The petals and the dirt, and the multiple light
On the smooth trunk.
They run almost like palpable hares,
Inspecting the imaginary hill, dark,
Full of mandrake, full of weightlessness,
And they stop for many minutes,
And the centuries seem to matter
Only when they play among the unmasked Earth.

CXXIII

Flame of the fire,
Tall perpendicular sun,
The sapling grows high on the flame's edge,
And the warm wet birds fly
Through the sun's white glare,
And we partake in this warm span
That turns hot then green.
We reach for the dry green span
That turns into a cool silvery brook,
And the dry white birds
Land vertically above our heads,
With mandibles up,
We see the sphere-like flame, gray,
Behind the transparent veil.

CXXIV

The town is marble white,
And the icicles are ivory tusks,
And the wilderness is snowbound.
A blizzard fell quietly
From the calm black sky,
And overnight, a natural white painted the morning
            eyes,
And the people remember their instinctive past,
And the animals remember their hunger and thirst,
And the blinding frost subsides
Into an ocherous vision.
The people become settlers in their own vicinity.
The animals feast upon the boundless seasons.

CXXV

Far from the inaudible voice
And village cloud,
The rain still falls
Until the descent stops upon the resident beast,
But there is still a vague descent in the day,
Spoken voices among the afternoon trees,
And we hear our own particle of sound
Among the sounds other than our own.
We speak to each other before the silence,
Before it begins,
Before the end of the beautiful sounds,
And we speak to our sounds
As a particle of life,
As an audible voice.

CXXVI

She offers me an acorn,
And life is here,
And the fallen leaves nourish the earth,
And the great white oak
Rubs against the infinite space.
She reclines with her breasts
Against the blue complexion of the sky,
And I kiss the blue light on her lips,
The fallen oak nourishes the time,
And life is here, everywhere,
Among the pulsation of air.
She feels the heart pulse in my chest,
And I squeeze the acorn in my hand.

CXXVII

Behind green flowers and wind,
The old couple embrace the many years
They walked beyond the uncertain past.
They hold the green wind
Beyond their newborn hands,
And the old woman tells the old man with her eyes,
And he waits, happily, with tears in his eyes
For time and the sun,
And she waits with him under the newborn day.
They rise each day under the east
And embrace the beauty beyond the years.

CXXVIII

Tawny fish,
Shy in its liquid world,
Great fish,
As old as the silver glaciers,
With eyes like black mirrors,
Reflecting our terrestrial world,
And the sun leaves its orange print
On the roof of their subaqueous home,
And the blue and white boats
Sail in all directions to use their private world,
Their beautiful world, unknown,
As old as the tawny earth,
As clear as the full moon,
And as deep as the human imagination.

CXXIX

Who said the Milky Way is our galaxy?
But we speak and make love
Under this galaxy.
But we listen and observe
Under a different sun.
We sleep and dream under the dark light-years.
And the insect bends its antennae
Over a microscopic world.
I am with her, flesh upon flesh,
Above all that falls upon this surface.
I turn, her mouth parted, recumbent hair,
Lids like white petals, lashes still,
She dreams our night under the lucent moon.

CXXX

Black and yellow flock,
And a goldfinch grazes the perforated wind,
Three seasons pass this dormant house,
The weather and the wings are like the wind,
They pass through gaping wood and open windows,
And the house still has those black wings,
A gathering for an indoor breeze
And oscillating feathers,
A rare view from the summer hill,
The nests closed with shade and snow,
The fourth season strokes the sky with color,
And the leaves flock brown and green.

CXXXI

Music of strings and chirps
Sounds like the lyre,
But the nearest mountains
Sound like a distant flute,
And far away, the rain falls from the sky,
And the rainwater falls lightly
On feathers and strings,
The brittle wetness crumbles onto the saturated grove,
As the melody shapes the mute horizon,
And the timeless cries of embedded life
Reshape the human ear,
Or people on their solitary walks
Find the musical rain beautiful or unreal.

CXXXII

Space and the hoary world,
And the bright stones are the stars of Earth,
And Jupiter rises bright against black
On the dark blue.
I know its immensity,
But we cannot see its Great Red Spot.
I know its beauty,
But we cannot see its four visible moons.
We see the crisp evening trees rise black
Like an illusionary star,
And the dark blue reality rises south
In formation with bands of colors
Or crickets and bats.

CXXXIII

Tiny moth, brown,
Flutters from sunshine to shade
Back to sunshine,
Then thunder passes and lightning delays
As a beating heart remains below the flashing gray,
Beating between the sound and the light,
A time measured without a device,
A measurement of the mind,
Hand upon the breast,
And sunlight between the fingers,
The crowd of dark flowers
Emitting a mountainous scent,
And the crowd of shade surrounds the top,
As the heart beats in the brown light.

CXXXIV

I dreamt of the blue sky,
And she dreamt of the white sky,
We dream that the moon has green trees,
And the moon's clouds shed bright rain on its face,
And the bobolink's last flight
Finds the moon's troposphere.
We awake among ourselves,
With our flesh clear with moisture, like glass,
Like the world's ancient lakes,
Like a blue and white transparency
Seen deep behind the daylight vision,
A profound sleep.

CXXXV

The water specks that exist with invisibility
Exist as a tangible glare,
And there is a new moon above the old tree,
And the strangers try to measure the absent light
And the unseen bark,
They move with certainty
Among the dead twigs,
But they hear its life communicating
In the thick fire,
The sole fire makes low sounds,
A crackling voice, wild and primitive,
And the strangers dry their clothes
And warm their hands,
They watch the burnt air and timeless speech.

CXXXVI

How many times has the moon been full?
How many times has the moon fulfilled
Its partial phases?
And the lost tales of the fox and the sun
Form in the children's memory,
And written proof of the white owl,
Like snow in flight,
Forms before the children's eyes,
And the true stories of dusk
Become morning legends,
A role the children live in the forest
And in the town, a future fable,
Beautifully told of marsh blue violets
And dust around the gibbous phase.

CXXXVII

The guest knows we are lovers,
And I walk her down
To where the butterflies rest,
Where an indigo ring shines around
The mane-like shrubs and tresses of light,
Shredded in green,
Hanging down before the butterflies eat,
And the guest passes through the untold scenes,
Leaving visions and prints,
Leaving the town and a patch of nature,
And we notice the absence,
And we notice the omnipotent host,
And we see the guest return
To visit statues and trees.

CXXXVIII

They are the violins of the trees,
And the redbirds vibrate those strings.
The leaves rub those strings,
And there is the sound of the zither.
The heavens drip,
And in time form those green ponds.
Gray logs burn in a hearthstone,
And in time the smoke ascends then dissipates,
And the old farmer plays his mandolin
For the redbirds,
And seconds before or thousands of years with song,
The dawn beckons like a cithara.

CXXXIX

Hands and azure,
Blue light in fingers and palms,
She holds it like half a rose, yellow,
Golden between sun and stone,
Distant between stratosphere and shore,
Soft on her breast,
Life on bare seeds,
And the view from above, with a force or an eye,
With reality and nakedness,
And her vaporous hands, solid, gentle,
Warm on my face and hands,
Eyes closed, feeling for the sky,
Distinguishing flesh, colors, and light,
Seeing each other, seeing the entire rose.

CXL

You can actually hear the day being born.
And the gray moose, scarce,
Is compared to the brown eclipse,
It becomes dark and swiftly fades like May frost,
And the golden petals
Bask in their own reflections,
Scarce, yellow, and bright,
A stable degree of tint that mixes antlers and stems,
A shedding process that mixes weight and growth,
And a deep bright puff,
Buried loud behind the highest ground,
Submerged in the dark air.

CXLI

The shade begins peeling at the surface,
But my eyes always return to her
And to the first layer of earth
Far beneath our resting eyes,
But my heart always feels the time,
And she is always part of what I see,
And always that part between water and sky,
The connection between surface and shade,
The part between swans and eagles,
The whole dimension of sandstones and sunspots,
Or the beautiful trace of her existence.

CXLII

The first signs of a closing night
Remind me of a green medley,
And after dreaming in the break of light,
The shadows stay with us
Until Mercury climbs in yellow and orange,
Keeping the same hot visage toward the youthful sun,
And the first signs of dawn
Remind me of a yellow overture,
And we both witness the escalating haze,
Like a dust-filled galaxy,
Like a silver foam,
Or turning like the youthful hair,
Combed in the break of dusk.

CXLIII

And in front of the green well,
The strangers collect fresh water.
Black duck near the green birds.
Boats sail for the land.
The wetlands solidify at the dark gray stump.
Liquescent eyes watch from aqueous rocks,
And in front of the old concave road,
The strangers meditate on a withered field.
Frequent years beyond inseparable hours.
The external world tells time,
Bringing in everything and the primitive mind.
Beauty and simplicity on prostrate earth.
Corner and center,
The strangers predict their tracks.

CXLIV

She is like the crescent east,
Like the song sparrow,
Soft, in the hidden birch,
She always sees the impalpable light on my eyes,
And the blind glare in my flesh,
She kisses me under the naked sun,
Naked lips to shaded lips,
This shaded sun is so warm,
And this naked breeze licks her eyes and flesh,
I hold this naked breeze against my heart,
And her body peers from the crescent sun,
She is the beauty in the hidden song.

CXLV

Let me wander in her reclining light,
Let me follow her unconditional heart,
Let the pools of wings and mist
Surround her gentle aura,
Let the subtle years grow
Into absolute days,
And the many seconds turn this bare beauty
Into a green sphere,
The minutes collect the vast treasures of time,
The human clock moves around mortal hands,
An inherent orbit around original days,
An inborn touch of the reclining heart,
But let me dwell in her gentle aura.

CXLVI

And the golden gills breathe
Beneath Earth's solitary moon,
The silver scales reflect the moon's sunlight,
The fish's eyes watch the surface of the moon.
They see us in half,
Like a half-screened tree,
Like a curtain of green leaves.
They see us with scented water on our skin.
They see us with rainwater on our tongues,
And we watch the whole morning side,
Half moon, half leaves,
And she forms my brow with sweet flowering light,
I reciprocate in the darkness.

CXLVII

Hickory gray,
Tall, noiseless, age unknown,
A product of wind and seeds,
A creature of roots and limbs,
Wildcat brown, small, noiseless, age unknown,
A product of rain and secrecy,
A creature, unique, with skin like bark,
Running through the woods,
Shedding its colors,
Preying on water, preying on meat,
A metamorphosis of green, brown, and gray,
A beautiful cycle of plant and beast,
A noiseless age,
Known only for its sound among plants and beasts.

CXLVIII

The guest spends time
With the mountain, the sun, the lake,
And stops to hear the magnificent eggs,
Unhatched, still, grayish-white with brown spots,
And the guest waits by the breaking shells,
Watching for the host, watching the change
In the immediate white, watching everything change
From beyond the four seasons,
Listening past the empty shells,
Feeling for its omnipresence,
Feeling the time span,
And the guest thinks of the precious boundaries on Earth.

CXLIX

She sleeps uncovered in my dreams,
And I cover her flesh with twinkling flowers,
I arouse her with a mute kiss,
She wakes me with a quiet embrace,
And she lies in the sepals and the stars,
And nature takes its course,
But we imagine asleep, a reality of dreams,
Conscious of microcosms blooming in our thoughts,
White dust from the comet
Passes over the green grass,
Conscious of macrocosms shrinking on our sleep,
And she covers herself with my dreams.

CL

Near a hilltop,
Close to their home,
The old woman appears as the maiden,
And the old man follows her to their piece of earth,
And the hilltop grows wrinkled and white,
A hoary mix of beauty and time,
A gray road close to their home,
Scattered with green and white petals,
Like a glowing powder from yellow suns,
And near a starling, close to their home,
The old man meets with the old woman,
They reflect, they relive their lives,
They live with joy, the reflections of time.

CLI

Scarlet tanager,
A figment of frost,
Black and red in the breast of clouds,
Or the years of June hover
Like the blue jays of March,
And the bent limbs move like vertical arms,
Reaching higher than the level of sails,
But the whitecaps never form,
Instead, a guttural sound forms from the waves,
And a ray of water, bright, dry of color,
Forms a figment of air,
And settles upon the exact selection,
And, again, the years turn into what the whole day has
        left.

CLII

The wing holds daylight in its vast embrace,
Neptune holds its moons,
Mars holds its moons,
The exosphere holds the new moon, black,
Between soil and space,
Or a bright orange field, of butterfly weeds,
Holds the humid scent of temperate months,
And the mysterious hands under evening,
White skin, blue veins,
Have an ancient hold on Earth,
A burning grasp of flowing lakes,
A flashing clutch of dark rock,
And the last release,
Like black feathers under the evening palm.

CLIII

The woodwinds play
And call in the circle of children,
They follow the wind-blown sound
And music of the past,
They listen among the old black trees,
Centuries of unrecorded time,
Minutes from the ripe August fruit.
But the children respond from a different circle,
An encircling beauty full of mammals and maples,
A formative life flowering in the mud or the moon,
A song sung only by the children,
Heard from the mouth of a little stream,
Or the piper of woodwinds.

CLIV

No prints, no tracks,
The snow like a calm white sea,
Like the milky lake
Over black rocks or dark earth.
February or December,
The first or the last storm,
The white face melts into a dark impression,
It sees and it speaks, white eyes, white lips,
The dark wing freezes into a pale immersion,
But the flight can be seen and told by many,
An old story of the dark and the white,
A wintry month, or no signs or indications
On the forgotten ground.

CLV

Death occurs and life begins,
Greens of life, yellows of death,
My heart lives between the greenish-yellow,
And in the palm or the light-year,
My heart beats from sky to sky,
And the stone and the tree beat continuously
Until the end of the terrestrial light,
And the fish and the birds
Have their hearts among the orbicular world,
And the rainwater settles below
The green and yellow arc,
Moving westward between the inclined slope
And Sirius rising.

CLVI

Can the raven's eye observe Saturn
In the daylight's shade?
Can the white pigments of night
Reflect Titan or its blackness?
And why does the fire from black leaves
Resemble the pallor of snow and fog?
Is this an epoch of a human mind
Or a minute of nature?
Are these the familiar rings
Or is this the strange moon?
And the last dry leaf falls white
In the first beautiful flame,
And the last cloudless thunder
Sounds pale in the first beautiful rain.

CLVII

She poses for me under the yellow bough,
The bright yellow sunlight engulfs her hands and feet,
Her breasts blossom through the twilight trees,
And the dark blue breeze transforms her hair,
I visualize the lovely scent in the parted breeze,
I lie on my side facing the parted sun,
We smell the light of dusk being born,
We kiss the sparkle of dawn lifting above,
She lies on her side facing my eyes,
And the yellow bough is now white with starlight.

CLVIII

Soil, lightning, and water,
This is what the strangers spoke about
In the quaint little town,
A town unmeasured from the connecting woods,
But measured from the unseen wilderness,
As a marsh hawk skims the top
Of the striped blue marshes.
But the town hears the unsettled glide,
An identical sound from the connecting woods,
And the strangers speak of the wilderness,
And they speak of the days before the town,
Before the conglomerations,
Before the highest production.

CLIX

Ants can roam for hours in the light,
And a small white hand
Can shade them for hours,
And in all these auburn trees,
The light leaps like a bright yellow frog,
And the children leap like a bright yellow light,
And the hot days melt the white shades,
And the cold nights freeze the brown lights.
But the children conclude, after the return,
That the hours are like the savage vines,
Full of bursts and colors,
No difference in seconds and years,
No difference in clocks and comets.

CLX

The soft gray mountain fades piecemeal into my mind
Spreading the blue waters across my eyes.
I hold the light of waters,
She holds the white moonlight,
And we bathe in the moist black air,
And above our upturned eyes,
Open to the smallest blaze
Are Mars and Saturn,
Open to the grayish-day air,
Open to the gray jay and the mockingbird,
Close to the fading waters,
And we touch the ground fading for centuries
Below the contiguous heavens.

CLXI

The house has its windows, table, and fireplace,
The rooms have their view,
The house is separated from view,
Between night pine and mountain ash,
The blue river flows west
Along the summer stones,
And in this house,
The ear can distinguish color from sound,
The rooms seem to grow outward,
Level with the outside world,
Level with the vast perimeters,
Level with each distinct species,
And the house has its guest,
A cogitative guest exploring every room,
And a temporary view of the outside world.

CLXII

Sun crystals and the cloud's horizon solidify and blend,
Casting a stone hue at the bottom of all water,
At the height of all snow,
At the crossing of all orbits,
And the ice-out or the sunlight
Formulates the time pattern,
And the discoidal mark in heaven's night
Formulates a clear star or the Stone Age.
A transparency rests on all
Bark, skin, limbs, arms,
And brown roots, like veins in feet,
Become blue in the open space
Where the guests can walk.

CLXIII

Fire and the moon.
Water and the sun.
Where is the palpability between fire and water?
How does the philosophy intervene
With the night or the trees?
And all the satellites and all the stars
Outweigh the flame and the flood,
But the corner has its blue and orange space,
The corner for the infinite bird,
A space for the one world,
Twinflowers growing in the same space,
That one bird concealed
As the color of the sun
And the shape of the moon.

CLXIV

That voice of the black rocks,
That voice of light,
She tells me to listen to its pale sequence,
And we combine our voices
Among ravens and suns,
And we are white like the tree,
Visible and delicate against its enormous leaves,
And she cradles my hands in its fruits and bareness,
And the old sequence shows its voice
Day after day like a vocal tinge
Against slumber and sky,
And we cradle the vision in its beauty
As the odor of moon lowers its gray scent.

CLXV

Years from the open eggs and mature wombs,
And the guests weep with joy
Below the stars' aroma,
And life or death takes any shape
Among the clarity of clouds,
The clear sleep unbroken
Below the interim of perpetual orbits,
And the guests think in time
About the impermanent dreams,
And the journey continues with that river
Of grass flowing east,
Green outside the consciousness of nearby minds,
And the visitors are the guests,
And the interim is itself the years.

CLXVI

My own thoughts inquire
About the nature of an unknown philosophy,
But our simple explanations satisfy the beating heart,
And we listen to the words
Spoken with an ancient tongue,
Making the first word
A warm white moonlight on experiential hearts,
The first experience of an eclipse,
The total light fading whole,
Bright, invisible, returning as the mortal heart,
Beating against the foreign light,
Pure, like the pre-dawn suns,
Spilling their bright yellow nights
On our light blue world.

CLXVII

O light,
Filtered vast through the pale wind
Like a coral night, no petals, no rain,
Like a flower of skin and tears,
Like the perspiration from flesh,
Like the human part of animated seeds,
And behold, pale sun,
Blinding beauty among the internal worlds,
An external implosion of silence,
Of light-years, like butterflies under the pears,
Or children under the day,
And the winding path inclines
Toward the base of the fog,
A vertical scene from the host of our entire planet.

CLXVIII

The crow speaks like the dark rain,
But we sleep among the night,
We are awake,
She peers through the moon like the eastern pupils,
Her eyes rise up like the eastern light,
I face the moon,
I speak among the dark rain,
The brightest blue grows dim with beauty,
We are conscious of the future and the past,
But the speech is still mute
Like music from the trillionth sun,
Bending close to our tongue and our ear.

CLXIX

I long for her hands upon my heart,
I long for the interval of this amber tree,
She presses her hands lightly upon my bosom,
She loves me among the unconditional leaves.
And the expectancy of life flourishes among the interval
        itself
As the hanging light of Venus,
Or a magnifying glass hanging between intervals
Of galaxies and grains.
And we long for our limitary time,
The breath of another day,
From sunrise to sunset,
From black soil to white sky,
From the last beat of the hanging heart.

CLXX

In what dimension of sky
Does Mars rise in its obvious shape?
And in what sky does the dimension of Andromeda
Rise in its oblivious color?
And the first human eye
Could see that tiny black and yellow bird
Move from twig to bough to trunk,
And the slow-moving sky is now purple and blue,
Rising above the first formation of water and land,
A dry drop from the colorless shape,
No one at this time
To behold the original beauty,
But the children sleep peacefully among this time.

CLXXI

The guest sits patiently
Among thorns and petals,
Waiting for the night to change,
Waiting for the permanent day,
Waiting for permission among the dark and the light.
The guest walks respectfully upon stones and soil,
Waiting for thoughts to change,
Greeting that soft white moonlight,
Welcoming that pale yellow sunshine.
And the guest bows before the host,
Accepting the harsh day and the temperate night,
Accepting the inevitable wing,
Accepting the inevitable fin,
A permanent change began subtly.

CLXXII

I have her face within my hands,
Lips and breasts upon my flesh,
Red and white upon my flesh,
I kiss the first sound of words,
I kiss the first drop of milk,
I feel her complexion within my hands,
Warm, like the golden sun,
And we feel the life, the breath, and the heartbeats
Between the earth and the stars,
And the night sways in blue and black,
In absolute stillness, and I reach my hands
Among the infinite and the flesh.

CLXXIII

A pure white galaxy
Seen through eyes from a tall green tree,
And the distant hills reflect the green and white sky,
And the mammals breathe the distant air,
And the brown bird resembles its ancestors,
And the pioneers resemble their reflections.
The mirror-like sun,
The yellow reflections on the pure white water,
And the pioneers peer at themselves from long, long ago,
They realize through clouded eyes
A visual perception, clear,
Of darkness and the ancient world,
Through beauty and beasts alike.

CLXXIV

We hear the magnificent calm within
Thunder, rain, and wind,
We feel the wind caress our arms and legs,
We taste the rain on our palates and lips,
We smell the thunder upon saturated earth,
We think among the populated void,
The multitude of sky,
The empty spaces of white,
A total blackness around bright Saturn and orange
                    flowers,
A strange plain of beauty calls to us
Like the stirring of petals or the moving of planets,
And we imagine,
And we become the first tree and the last cloud.

CLXXV

In the soft hues of the growing light,
The old man sees the old woman
Smiling in that growing light.
Black and white birds flock in different hues,
The star of day burns orange
Against the blue and white sky,
And the old woman extends a gentle hand
Toward the old man,
And that moon-like sun casts shadows of beauty
Like bright birds among the twilight of dawn,
And they embrace for the first time
In the hues of life,
Like the first transformation of light.

CLXXVI

Imagine this vastness among the solitary grain,
Or the apple trees against the trillion skies.
Imagine the water and the wind,
Warm like the rising sun,
And the imagination of the songbird,
Singing among the yellow clouds,
A vast image of night and day,
Blending into a soft light gray,
A beautiful sound like the snow and the solitary stars,
Or a deep figure embedded among
The rain and the imagination,
An evolution of colors changing in the shades of white.

CLXXVII

Let us not weep for the dead,
And let us weep not for the dying star
Light-years from our eyes,
And let us weep not for the human heart
Beating in the depths of darkness and tranquility,
But let us weep for the beauty
Of the mortal sun
And the yellow light that it sheds.
Let us think among the distant minds,
The purity of darkness
And the depths of beauty,
The absent flash of infinity,
The energy of two,
And the tears that separate among the living.

CLXXVIII

Water and stars mix in our hands,
Space and thoughts separate in our minds,
We dream because we live,
We live among the omnipotent light,
We live among blinding blackness and universal white,
We pause before the first sound,
It is as if a petal falls in our sleep,
Landing in our hands,
And in our thoughts we pause
Before the wetness and the warmth,
A dream of the warm, wet earth,
A life of beauty among the separate sounds,
And the mixture of death and life.

CLXXIX

In the light of the soft scent she wakes,
And I love her
Among all the tears and all the beauty,
And we peer together
Through the brightest day at the lightless rock,
It is the foundation of Earth,
It is the original blackness
Sharing life with the brilliant specks,
And the mortal trees breathe the finite air,
And the endless lights of blues and whites
Shine upon this dormant black,
But we peer together in life
Among sky and Earth.

CLXXX

It seems I can never write enough
Under the eastern sun,
But I can think among the infinity,
And the western sky has its peripheral hue,
And the abstract tints rotate words and thoughts,
And the grayness becomes its own palpability,
But the seasons are like atoms in space,
A vast thought of Earth's void,
A white petal, a white snowflake,
A blackbird becomes a distant beauty,
And the eastern sun, a distant white,
Beautiful, rotates with day and night,
And I write among the infinity.

CLXXXI

And the first season settles quietly
Below the first sky,
What birds! What comets!
Wings and tails reflect against the morning moon,
The swelling sun sets
Above the soft gray night,
Earth's flora and fauna
Reflect against Venus and Mars,
I reflect upon life and death,
The guests reflect upon life and death,
I am only a guest among the seasons,
I am only a guest below the sky,
And the first guest reflects upon the last season.

CLXXXII

Leaf and lake are the shape of the heavens,
The first shadow is of creatures and sun,
And the first light of the moon,
Beautiful, against her shaded face,
We share the first light,
We are guests among life and darkness,
I bathe her womb in the light,
I bathe her breasts in that bright yellow shade,
The stars shape her face against my sleeping eyes,
Silently the heavens awake the life and the void,
And the first light of day,
Beautiful, against leaf and lake.

CLXXXIII

Black hole,
A white wing soaring into Earth's whiteness,
Soil, crust, and dirt
Now part of the universe,
And the vast specks twinkling bright
Behind every sun and every moon,
And the invisible rose blooms red
In every crater and every chasm,
And the host beckons
With a gentle hand and primordial words,
Like a speck upon the rose,
Twinkling upon Earth, visible below the cloud,
And the white bird, like an apex of light,
Soaring and twinkling in the black hole.

CLXXXIV

Matter,
Colorless, odorless, and tasteless,
An omnipresence of life and death.
A colorless star
Seen through the light-years of human eyes.
The odorless sky
Stretched among the corners of infinity.
The tasteless night
Absorbed beyond the continuity of day.
The children follow the black stones
And the white light of the moon.
The guests respond with timeless rocks
And brilliant suns,
They respond with consciousness and imagination,
They respond to the dreams of children
With the thoughts and the palpability of matter.